addresses

PETER PAUPER PRESS, INC.
WHITE PLAINS, NEW YORK

PETER PAUPER PRESS

Fine Books and Gifts Since 1928

Our Company

In 1928, at the age of twenty-two, Peter Beilenson began printing books on a small press in the basement of his parents' home in Larchmont, New York. Peter—and later, his wife, Edna—sought to create fine books that sold at "prices even a pauper could afford."

Today, still family owned and operated, Peter Pauper Press continues to honor our founders' legacy—and our customers' expectations—of beauty, quality, and value.

Cover image by Wendy MacFarlane for Jane Mosse Designs

202 Mamaroneck Avenue
White Plains, NY 10601

ISBN 978-1-59359-223-3
Printed in Hong Kong
35 34 33 32

Visit us at www.peterpauper.com

addresses

NAME

ADDRESS

HOME

MOBILE

WORK / FAX

E-MAIL

NAME

ADDRESS

HOME

MOBILE

WORK / FAX

E-MAIL

NAME

ADDRESS

HOME

MOBILE

WORK / FAX

E-MAIL

NAME

ADDRESS

HOME

MOBILE

WORK / FAX

E-MAIL

NAME

ADDRESS

HOME

MOBILE

WORK / FAX

E-MAIL

NAME

ADDRESS

HOME

MOBILE

WORK / FAX

E-MAIL

NAME

ADDRESS

HOME

MOBILE

WORK / FAX

E-MAIL

NAME

ADDRESS

HOME

MOBILE

WORK / FAX

E-MAIL

NAME

ADDRESS

HOME

MOBILE

WORK / FAX

E-MAIL

NAME

ADDRESS

HOME

MOBILE

WORK / FAX

E-MAIL

NAME

ADDRESS

HOME

MOBILE

WORK / FAX

E-MAIL

NAME

ADDRESS

HOME

MOBILE

WORK / FAX

E-MAIL

NAME

ADDRESS

HOME

MOBILE

WORK / FAX

E-MAIL

NAME

ADDRESS

HOME

MOBILE

WORK / FAX

E-MAIL

NAME

ADDRESS

HOME

MOBILE

WORK / FAX

E-MAIL

Name

Address

Home

Mobile

Work / Fax

E-Mail

Name

Address

Home

Mobile

Work / Fax

E-Mail

Name

Address

Home

Mobile

Work / Fax

E-Mail

NAME

ADDRESS

HOME

MOBILE

WORK / FAX

E-MAIL

NAME

ADDRESS

HOME

MOBILE

WORK / FAX

E-MAIL

NAME

ADDRESS

HOME

MOBILE

WORK / FAX

E-MAIL

NAME

ADDRESS

HOME

MOBILE

WORK / FAX

E-MAIL

NAME

ADDRESS

HOME

MOBILE

WORK / FAX

E-MAIL

NAME

ADDRESS

HOME

MOBILE

WORK / FAX

E-MAIL

NAME

ADDRESS

HOME

MOBILE

WORK / FAX

E-MAIL

NAME

ADDRESS

HOME

MOBILE

WORK / FAX

E-MAIL

NAME

ADDRESS

HOME

MOBILE

WORK / FAX

E-MAIL

Name

Address

Home

Mobile

Work / Fax

E-Mail

Name

Address

Home

Mobile

Work / Fax

E-Mail

Name

Address

Home

Mobile

Work / Fax

E-Mail

NAME

ADDRESS

HOME

MOBILE

WORK / FAX

E-MAIL

NAME

ADDRESS

HOME

MOBILE

WORK / FAX

E-MAIL

NAME

ADDRESS

HOME

MOBILE

WORK / FAX

E-MAIL

NAME

ADDRESS

HOME

MOBILE

WORK / FAX

E-MAIL

NAME

ADDRESS

HOME

MOBILE

WORK / FAX

E-MAIL

NAME

ADDRESS

HOME

MOBILE

WORK / FAX

E-MAIL

NAME

ADDRESS

HOME

MOBILE

WORK / FAX

E-MAIL

NAME

ADDRESS

HOME

MOBILE

WORK / FAX

E-MAIL

NAME

ADDRESS

HOME

MOBILE

WORK / FAX

E-MAIL

NAME

ADDRESS

HOME

MOBILE

WORK / FAX

E-MAIL

NAME

ADDRESS

HOME

MOBILE

WORK / FAX

E-MAIL

NAME

ADDRESS

HOME

MOBILE

WORK / FAX

E-MAIL

NAME

ADDRESS

HOME

MOBILE

WORK / FAX

E-MAIL

NAME

ADDRESS

HOME

MOBILE

WORK / FAX

E-MAIL

NAME

ADDRESS

HOME

MOBILE

WORK / FAX

E-MAIL

Name

Address

Home

Mobile

Work / Fax

E-Mail

Name

Address

Home

Mobile

Work / Fax

E-Mail

Name

Address

Home

Mobile

Work / Fax

E-Mail

NAME

ADDRESS

HOME

MOBILE

WORK / FAX

E-MAIL

NAME

ADDRESS

HOME

MOBILE

WORK / FAX

E-MAIL

NAME

ADDRESS

HOME

MOBILE

WORK / FAX

E-MAIL

NAME

ADDRESS

HOME

MOBILE

WORK / FAX

E-MAIL

NAME

ADDRESS

HOME

MOBILE

WORK / FAX

E-MAIL

NAME

ADDRESS

HOME

MOBILE

WORK / FAX

E-MAIL

NAME

ADDRESS

HOME

MOBILE

WORK / FAX

E-MAIL

NAME

ADDRESS

HOME

MOBILE

WORK / FAX

E-MAIL

NAME

ADDRESS

HOME

MOBILE

WORK / FAX

E-MAIL

NAME

ADDRESS

HOME

MOBILE

WORK / FAX

E-MAIL

NAME

ADDRESS

HOME

MOBILE

WORK / FAX

E-MAIL

NAME

ADDRESS

HOME

MOBILE

WORK / FAX

E-MAIL

NAME

ADDRESS

HOME

MOBILE

WORK / FAX

E-MAIL

NAME

ADDRESS

HOME

MOBILE

WORK / FAX

E-MAIL

NAME

ADDRESS

HOME

MOBILE

WORK / FAX

E-MAIL

NAME

ADDRESS

HOME

MOBILE

WORK / FAX

E-MAIL

NAME

ADDRESS

HOME

MOBILE

WORK / FAX

E-MAIL

NAME

ADDRESS

HOME

MOBILE

WORK / FAX

E-MAIL

C
D

NAME

ADDRESS

HOME

MOBILE

WORK / FAX

E-MAIL

NAME

ADDRESS

HOME

MOBILE

WORK / FAX

E-MAIL

NAME

ADDRESS

HOME

MOBILE

WORK / FAX

E-MAIL

NAME

ADDRESS

HOME

MOBILE

WORK / FAX

E-MAIL

NAME

ADDRESS

HOME

MOBILE

WORK / FAX

E-MAIL

NAME

ADDRESS

HOME

MOBILE

WORK / FAX

E-MAIL

NAME

ADDRESS

HOME

MOBILE

WORK / FAX

E-MAIL

NAME

ADDRESS

HOME

MOBILE

WORK / FAX

E-MAIL

NAME

ADDRESS

HOME

MOBILE

WORK / FAX

E-MAIL

NAME

ADDRESS

HOME

MOBILE

WORK / FAX

E-MAIL

NAME

ADDRESS

HOME

MOBILE

WORK / FAX

E-MAIL

NAME

ADDRESS

HOME

MOBILE

WORK / FAX

E-MAIL

NAME

ADDRESS

HOME

MOBILE

WORK / FAX

E-MAIL

NAME

ADDRESS

HOME

MOBILE

WORK / FAX

E-MAIL

NAME

ADDRESS

HOME

MOBILE

WORK / FAX

E-MAIL

NAME

ADDRESS

HOME

MOBILE

WORK / FAX

E-MAIL

NAME

ADDRESS

HOME

MOBILE

WORK / FAX

E-MAIL

NAME

ADDRESS

HOME

MOBILE

WORK / FAX

E-MAIL

NAME

ADDRESS

HOME

MOBILE

WORK / FAX

E-MAIL

NAME

ADDRESS

HOME

MOBILE

WORK / FAX

E-MAIL

NAME

ADDRESS

HOME

MOBILE

WORK / FAX

E-MAIL

NAME

ADDRESS

HOME

MOBILE

WORK / FAX

E-MAIL

NAME

ADDRESS

HOME

MOBILE

WORK / FAX

E-MAIL

NAME

ADDRESS

HOME

MOBILE

WORK / FAX

E-MAIL

NAME

ADDRESS

HOME

MOBILE

WORK / FAX

E-MAIL

NAME

ADDRESS

HOME

MOBILE

WORK / FAX

E-MAIL

NAME

ADDRESS

HOME

MOBILE

WORK / FAX

E-MAIL

NAME

ADDRESS

HOME

MOBILE

WORK / FAX

E-MAIL

NAME

ADDRESS

HOME

MOBILE

WORK / FAX

E-MAIL

NAME

ADDRESS

HOME

MOBILE

WORK / FAX

E-MAIL

E
F

NAME

ADDRESS

HOME

MOBILE

WORK / FAX

E-MAIL

NAME

ADDRESS

HOME

MOBILE

WORK / FAX

E-MAIL

NAME

ADDRESS

HOME

MOBILE

WORK / FAX

E-MAIL

Name

Address

Home

Mobile

Work / Fax

E-Mail

Name

Address

Home

Mobile

Work / Fax

E-Mail

Name

Address

Home

Mobile

Work / Fax

E-Mail

Name

Address

Home

Mobile

Work / Fax

E-Mail

Name

Address

Home

Mobile

Work / Fax

E-Mail

Name

Address

Home

Mobile

Work / Fax

E-Mail

NAME

ADDRESS

HOME

MOBILE

WORK / FAX

E-MAIL

NAME

ADDRESS

HOME

MOBILE

WORK / FAX

E-MAIL

NAME

ADDRESS

HOME

MOBILE

WORK / FAX

E-MAIL

Name

Address

Home

Mobile

Work / Fax

E-Mail

G
H

Name

Address

Home

Mobile

Work / Fax

E-Mail

Name

Address

Home

Mobile

Work / Fax

E-Mail

Name

Address

Home

Mobile

Work / Fax

E-Mail

Name

Address

Home

Mobile

Work / Fax

E-Mail

Name

Address

Home

Mobile

Work / Fax

E-Mail

Name

Address

Home

Mobile

Work / Fax

E-Mail

Name

Address

Home

Mobile

Work / Fax

E-Mail

Name

Address

Home

Mobile

Work / Fax

E-Mail

Name

Address

Home

Mobile

Work / Fax

E-Mail

Name

Address

Home

Mobile

Work / Fax

E-Mail

Name

Address

Home

Mobile

Work / Fax

E-Mail

NAME

ADDRESS

HOME

MOBILE

WORK / FAX

E-MAIL

NAME

ADDRESS

HOME

MOBILE

WORK / FAX

E-MAIL

NAME

ADDRESS

HOME

MOBILE

WORK / FAX

E-MAIL

NAME

ADDRESS

HOME

MOBILE

WORK / FAX

E-MAIL

NAME

ADDRESS

HOME

MOBILE

WORK / FAX

E-MAIL

NAME

ADDRESS

HOME

MOBILE

WORK / FAX

E-MAIL

NAME

ADDRESS

HOME

MOBILE

WORK / FAX

E-MAIL

NAME

ADDRESS

HOME

MOBILE

WORK / FAX

E-MAIL

NAME

ADDRESS

HOME

MOBILE

WORK / FAX

E-MAIL

Name

Address

Home

Mobile

Work / Fax

E-Mail

Name

Address

Home

Mobile

Work / Fax

E-Mail

Name

Address

Home

Mobile

Work / Fax

E-Mail

GH

NAME

ADDRESS

HOME

MOBILE

WORK / FAX

E-MAIL

NAME

ADDRESS

HOME

MOBILE

WORK / FAX

E-MAIL

NAME

ADDRESS

HOME

MOBILE

WORK / FAX

E-MAIL

NAME

ADDRESS

HOME

MOBILE

WORK / FAX

E-MAIL

NAME

ADDRESS

HOME

MOBILE

WORK / FAX

E-MAIL

NAME

ADDRESS

HOME

MOBILE

WORK / FAX

E-MAIL

NAME

ADDRESS

HOME

MOBILE

WORK / FAX

E-MAIL

NAME

ADDRESS

HOME

MOBILE

WORK / FAX

E-MAIL

NAME

ADDRESS

HOME

MOBILE

WORK / FAX

E-MAIL

NAME

ADDRESS

HOME

MOBILE

WORK / FAX

E-MAIL

NAME

ADDRESS

HOME

MOBILE

WORK / FAX

E-MAIL

NAME

ADDRESS

HOME

MOBILE

WORK / FAX

E-MAIL

NAME

ADDRESS

HOME

MOBILE

WORK / FAX

E-MAIL

NAME

ADDRESS

HOME

MOBILE

WORK / FAX

E-MAIL

NAME

ADDRESS

HOME

MOBILE

WORK / FAX

E-MAIL

I J

NAME

ADDRESS

HOME

MOBILE

WORK / FAX

E-MAIL

NAME

ADDRESS

HOME

MOBILE

WORK / FAX

E-MAIL

NAME

ADDRESS

HOME

MOBILE

WORK / FAX

E-MAIL

NAME

ADDRESS

HOME

MOBILE

WORK / FAX

E-MAIL

NAME

ADDRESS

HOME

MOBILE

WORK / FAX

E-MAIL

NAME

ADDRESS

HOME

MOBILE

WORK / FAX

E-MAIL

Name

Address

Home

Mobile

Work / Fax

E-Mail

Name

Address

Home

Mobile

Work / Fax

E-Mail

Name

Address

Home

Mobile

Work / Fax

E-Mail

NAME

ADDRESS

HOME

MOBILE

WORK / FAX

E-MAIL

NAME

ADDRESS

HOME

MOBILE

WORK / FAX

E-MAIL

NAME

ADDRESS

HOME

MOBILE

WORK / FAX

E-MAIL

NAME

ADDRESS

HOME

MOBILE

WORK / FAX

E-MAIL

NAME

ADDRESS

HOME

MOBILE

WORK / FAX

E-MAIL

NAME

ADDRESS

HOME

MOBILE

WORK / FAX

E-MAIL

NAME

ADDRESS

HOME

MOBILE

WORK / FAX

E-MAIL

NAME

ADDRESS

HOME

MOBILE

WORK / FAX

E-MAIL

NAME

ADDRESS

HOME

MOBILE

WORK / FAX

E-MAIL

Name

Address

Home

Mobile

Work / Fax

E-Mail

Name

Address

Home

Mobile

Work / Fax

E-Mail

Name

Address

Home

Mobile

Work / Fax

E-Mail

NAME

ADDRESS

HOME

MOBILE

WORK / FAX

E-MAIL

NAME

ADDRESS

HOME

MOBILE

WORK / FAX

E-MAIL

NAME

ADDRESS

HOME

MOBILE

WORK / FAX

E-MAIL

NAME

ADDRESS

HOME

MOBILE

WORK / FAX

E-MAIL

NAME

ADDRESS

HOME

MOBILE

WORK / FAX

E-MAIL

NAME

ADDRESS

HOME

MOBILE

WORK / FAX

E-MAIL

NAME

ADDRESS

HOME

MOBILE

WORK / FAX

E-MAIL

NAME

ADDRESS

HOME

MOBILE

WORK / FAX

E-MAIL

NAME

ADDRESS

HOME

MOBILE

WORK / FAX

E-MAIL

Name

Address

Home

Mobile

Work / Fax

E-Mail

Name

Address

Home

Mobile

Work / Fax

E-Mail

Name

Address

Home

Mobile

Work / Fax

E-Mail

Name

Address

Home

Mobile

Work / Fax

E-Mail

Name

Address

Home

Mobile

Work / Fax

E-Mail

Name

Address

Home

Mobile

Work / Fax

E-Mail

K
L

NAME

ADDRESS

HOME

MOBILE

WORK / FAX

E-MAIL

NAME

ADDRESS

HOME

MOBILE

WORK / FAX

E-MAIL

NAME

ADDRESS

HOME

MOBILE

WORK / FAX

E-MAIL

NAME

ADDRESS

HOME

MOBILE

WORK / FAX

E-MAIL

NAME

ADDRESS

HOME

MOBILE

WORK / FAX

E-MAIL

NAME

ADDRESS

HOME

MOBILE

WORK / FAX

E-MAIL

K
L

NAME

ADDRESS

HOME

MOBILE

WORK / FAX

E-MAIL

NAME

ADDRESS

HOME

MOBILE

WORK / FAX

E-MAIL

NAME

ADDRESS

HOME

MOBILE

WORK / FAX

E-MAIL

NAME

ADDRESS

HOME

MOBILE

WORK / FAX

E-MAIL

NAME

ADDRESS

HOME

MOBILE

WORK / FAX

E-MAIL

NAME

ADDRESS

HOME

MOBILE

WORK / FAX

E-MAIL

NAME

ADDRESS

HOME

MOBILE

WORK / FAX

E-MAIL

NAME

ADDRESS

HOME

MOBILE

WORK / FAX

E-MAIL

NAME

ADDRESS

HOME

MOBILE

WORK / FAX

E-MAIL

NAME

ADDRESS

HOME

MOBILE

WORK / FAX

E-MAIL

NAME

ADDRESS

HOME

MOBILE

WORK / FAX

E-MAIL

NAME

ADDRESS

HOME

MOBILE

WORK / FAX

E-MAIL

NAME

ADDRESS

HOME

MOBILE

WORK / FAX

E-MAIL

NAME

ADDRESS

HOME

MOBILE

WORK / FAX

E-MAIL

NAME

ADDRESS

HOME

MOBILE

WORK / FAX

E-MAIL

NAME

ADDRESS

HOME

MOBILE

WORK / FAX

E-MAIL

NAME

ADDRESS

HOME

MOBILE

WORK / FAX

E-MAIL

NAME

ADDRESS

HOME

MOBILE

WORK / FAX

E-MAIL

Name

Address

Home

Mobile

Work / Fax

E-Mail

Name

Address

Home

Mobile

Work / Fax

E-Mail

Name

Address

Home

Mobile

Work / Fax

E-Mail

NAME

ADDRESS

HOME

MOBILE

WORK / FAX

E-MAIL

NAME

ADDRESS

HOME

MOBILE

WORK / FAX

E-MAIL

NAME

ADDRESS

HOME

MOBILE

WORK / FAX

E-MAIL

K
L

Name

Address

Home

Mobile

Work / Fax

E-Mail

Name

Address

Home

Mobile

Work / Fax

E-Mail

Name

Address

Home

Mobile

Work / Fax

E-Mail

Name

Address

Home

Mobile

Work / Fax

E-Mail

Name

Address

Home

Mobile

Work / Fax

E-Mail

Name

Address

Home

Mobile

Work / Fax

E-Mail

NAME

ADDRESS

HOME

MOBILE

WORK / FAX

E-MAIL

NAME

ADDRESS

HOME

MOBILE

WORK / FAX

E-MAIL

NAME

ADDRESS

HOME

MOBILE

WORK / FAX

E-MAIL

NAME

ADDRESS

HOME

MOBILE

WORK / FAX

E-MAIL

NAME

ADDRESS

HOME

MOBILE

WORK / FAX

E-MAIL

NAME

ADDRESS

HOME

MOBILE

WORK / FAX

E-MAIL

NAME

ADDRESS

HOME

MOBILE

WORK / FAX

E-MAIL

NAME

ADDRESS

HOME

MOBILE

WORK / FAX

E-MAIL

NAME

ADDRESS

HOME

MOBILE

WORK / FAX

E-MAIL

NAME

ADDRESS

HOME

MOBILE

WORK / FAX

E-MAIL

NAME

ADDRESS

HOME

MOBILE

WORK / FAX

E-MAIL

NAME

ADDRESS

HOME

MOBILE

WORK / FAX

E-MAIL

NAME

ADDRESS

HOME

MOBILE

WORK / FAX

E-MAIL

NAME

ADDRESS

HOME

MOBILE

WORK / FAX

E-MAIL

NAME

ADDRESS

HOME

MOBILE

WORK / FAX

E-MAIL

NAME

ADDRESS

HOME

MOBILE

WORK / FAX

E-MAIL

NAME

ADDRESS

HOME

MOBILE

WORK / FAX

E-MAIL

NAME

ADDRESS

HOME

MOBILE

WORK / FAX

E-MAIL

NAME

ADDRESS

HOME

MOBILE

WORK / FAX

E-MAIL

NAME

ADDRESS

HOME

MOBILE

WORK / FAX

E-MAIL

NAME

ADDRESS

HOME

MOBILE

WORK / FAX

E-MAIL

NAME

ADDRESS

HOME

MOBILE

WORK / FAX

E-MAIL

NAME

ADDRESS

HOME

MOBILE

WORK / FAX

E-MAIL

NAME

ADDRESS

HOME

MOBILE

WORK / FAX

E-MAIL

NAME

ADDRESS

HOME

MOBILE

WORK / FAX

E-MAIL

NAME

ADDRESS

HOME

MOBILE

WORK / FAX

E-MAIL

NAME

ADDRESS

HOME

MOBILE

WORK / FAX

E-MAIL

NAME

ADDRESS

HOME

MOBILE

WORK / FAX

E-MAIL

NAME

ADDRESS

HOME

MOBILE

WORK / FAX

E-MAIL

NAME

ADDRESS

HOME

MOBILE

WORK / FAX

E-MAIL

NAME

ADDRESS

HOME

MOBILE

WORK / FAX

E-MAIL

NAME

ADDRESS

HOME

MOBILE

WORK / FAX

E-MAIL

NAME

ADDRESS

HOME

MOBILE

WORK / FAX

E-MAIL

NAME

ADDRESS

HOME

MOBILE

WORK / FAX

E-MAIL

NAME

ADDRESS

HOME

MOBILE

WORK / FAX

E-MAIL

NAME

ADDRESS

HOME

MOBILE

WORK / FAX

E-MAIL

Name

Address

Home

Mobile

Work / Fax

E-Mail

Name

Address

Home

Mobile

Work / Fax

E-Mail

Name

Address

Home

Mobile

Work / Fax

E-Mail

NAME

ADDRESS

HOME

MOBILE

WORK / FAX

E-MAIL

NAME

ADDRESS

HOME

MOBILE

WORK / FAX

E-MAIL

NAME

ADDRESS

HOME

MOBILE

WORK / FAX

E-MAIL

NAME

ADDRESS

HOME

MOBILE

WORK / FAX

E-MAIL

NAME

ADDRESS

HOME

MOBILE

WORK / FAX

E-MAIL

NAME

ADDRESS

HOME

MOBILE

WORK / FAX

E-MAIL

NAME

ADDRESS

HOME

MOBILE

WORK / FAX

E-MAIL

NAME

ADDRESS

HOME

MOBILE

WORK / FAX

E-MAIL

NAME

ADDRESS

HOME

MOBILE

WORK / FAX

E-MAIL

Name

Address

Home

Mobile

Work / Fax

E-Mail

Name

Address

Home

Mobile

Work / Fax

E-Mail

Name

Address

Home

Mobile

Work / Fax

E-Mail

NAME

ADDRESS

HOME

MOBILE

WORK / FAX

E-MAIL

NAME

ADDRESS

HOME

MOBILE

WORK / FAX

E-MAIL

NAME

ADDRESS

HOME

MOBILE

WORK / FAX

E-MAIL

NAME

ADDRESS

HOME

MOBILE

WORK / FAX

E-MAIL

NAME

ADDRESS

HOME

MOBILE

WORK / FAX

E-MAIL

NAME

ADDRESS

HOME

MOBILE

WORK / FAX

E-MAIL

NAME

ADDRESS

HOME

MOBILE

WORK / FAX

E-MAIL

NAME

ADDRESS

HOME

MOBILE

WORK / FAX

E-MAIL

NAME

ADDRESS

HOME

MOBILE

WORK / FAX

E-MAIL

NAME

ADDRESS

HOME

MOBILE

WORK / FAX

E-MAIL

NAME

ADDRESS

HOME

MOBILE

WORK / FAX

E-MAIL

NAME

ADDRESS

HOME

MOBILE

WORK / FAX

E-MAIL

NAME

ADDRESS

HOME

MOBILE

WORK / FAX

E-MAIL

NAME

ADDRESS

HOME

MOBILE

WORK / FAX

E-MAIL

NAME

ADDRESS

HOME

MOBILE

WORK / FAX

E-MAIL

O P

NAME

ADDRESS

HOME

MOBILE

WORK / FAX

E-MAIL

NAME

ADDRESS

HOME

MOBILE

WORK / FAX

E-MAIL

NAME

ADDRESS

HOME

MOBILE

WORK / FAX

E-MAIL

NAME

ADDRESS

HOME

MOBILE

WORK / FAX

E-MAIL

NAME

ADDRESS

HOME

MOBILE

WORK / FAX

E-MAIL

NAME

ADDRESS

HOME

MOBILE

WORK / FAX

E-MAIL

NAME

ADDRESS

HOME

MOBILE

WORK / FAX

E-MAIL

NAME

ADDRESS

HOME

MOBILE

WORK / FAX

E-MAIL

NAME

ADDRESS

HOME

MOBILE

WORK / FAX

E-MAIL

NAME

ADDRESS

HOME

MOBILE

WORK / FAX

E-MAIL

NAME

ADDRESS

HOME

MOBILE

WORK / FAX

E-MAIL

NAME

ADDRESS

HOME

MOBILE

WORK / FAX

E-MAIL

Q
R

NAME

ADDRESS

HOME

MOBILE

WORK / FAX

E-MAIL

NAME

ADDRESS

HOME

MOBILE

WORK / FAX

E-MAIL

NAME

ADDRESS

HOME

MOBILE

WORK / FAX

E-MAIL

NAME

ADDRESS

HOME

MOBILE

WORK / FAX

E-MAIL

NAME

ADDRESS

HOME

MOBILE

WORK / FAX

E-MAIL

NAME

ADDRESS

HOME

MOBILE

WORK / FAX

E-MAIL

Name

Address

Home

Mobile

Work / Fax

E-Mail

Name

Address

Home

Mobile

Work / Fax

E-Mail

Name

Address

Home

Mobile

Work / Fax

E-Mail

NAME

ADDRESS

HOME

MOBILE

WORK / FAX

E-MAIL

NAME

ADDRESS

HOME

MOBILE

WORK / FAX

E-MAIL

NAME

ADDRESS

HOME

MOBILE

WORK / FAX

E-MAIL

NAME

ADDRESS

HOME

MOBILE

WORK / FAX

E-MAIL

NAME

ADDRESS

HOME

MOBILE

WORK / FAX

E-MAIL

NAME

ADDRESS

HOME

MOBILE

WORK / FAX

E-MAIL

NAME

ADDRESS

HOME

MOBILE

WORK / FAX

E-MAIL

NAME

ADDRESS

HOME

MOBILE

WORK / FAX

E-MAIL

NAME

ADDRESS

HOME

MOBILE

WORK / FAX

E-MAIL

Q
R

Name

Address

Home

Mobile

Work / Fax

E-Mail

Name

Address

Home

Mobile

Work / Fax

E-Mail

Name

Address

Home

Mobile

Work / Fax

E-Mail

NAME

ADDRESS

HOME

MOBILE

WORK / FAX

E-MAIL

NAME

ADDRESS

HOME

MOBILE

WORK / FAX

E-MAIL

NAME

ADDRESS

HOME

MOBILE

WORK / FAX

E-MAIL

NAME

ADDRESS

HOME

MOBILE

WORK / FAX

E-MAIL

NAME

ADDRESS

HOME

MOBILE

WORK / FAX

E-MAIL

NAME

ADDRESS

HOME

MOBILE

WORK / FAX

E-MAIL

NAME

ADDRESS

HOME

MOBILE

WORK / FAX

E-MAIL

NAME

ADDRESS

HOME

MOBILE

WORK / FAX

E-MAIL

NAME

ADDRESS

HOME

MOBILE

WORK / FAX

E-MAIL

NAME

ADDRESS

HOME

MOBILE

WORK / FAX

E-MAIL

NAME

ADDRESS

HOME

MOBILE

WORK / FAX

E-MAIL

NAME

ADDRESS

HOME

MOBILE

WORK / FAX

E-MAIL

NAME

ADDRESS

HOME

MOBILE

WORK / FAX

E-MAIL

NAME

ADDRESS

HOME

MOBILE

WORK / FAX

E-MAIL

NAME

ADDRESS

HOME

MOBILE

WORK / FAX

E-MAIL

S
T

NAME

ADDRESS

HOME

MOBILE

WORK / FAX

E-MAIL

NAME

ADDRESS

HOME

MOBILE

WORK / FAX

E-MAIL

NAME

ADDRESS

HOME

MOBILE

WORK / FAX

E-MAIL

NAME

ADDRESS

HOME

MOBILE

WORK / FAX

E-MAIL

NAME

ADDRESS

HOME

MOBILE

WORK / FAX

E-MAIL

NAME

ADDRESS

HOME

MOBILE

WORK / FAX

E-MAIL

Name

Address

Home

Mobile

Work / Fax

E-Mail

Name

Address

Home

Mobile

Work / Fax

E-Mail

Name

Address

Home

Mobile

Work / Fax

E-Mail

NAME

ADDRESS

HOME

MOBILE

WORK / FAX

E-MAIL

NAME

ADDRESS

HOME

MOBILE

WORK / FAX

E-MAIL

NAME

ADDRESS

HOME

MOBILE

WORK / FAX

E-MAIL

NAME

ADDRESS

HOME

MOBILE

WORK / FAX

E-MAIL

NAME

ADDRESS

HOME

MOBILE

WORK / FAX

E-MAIL

NAME

ADDRESS

HOME

MOBILE

WORK / FAX

E-MAIL

NAME

ADDRESS

HOME

MOBILE

WORK / FAX

E-MAIL

NAME

ADDRESS

HOME

MOBILE

WORK / FAX

E-MAIL

NAME

ADDRESS

HOME

MOBILE

WORK / FAX

E-MAIL

NAME

ADDRESS

HOME

MOBILE

WORK / FAX

E-MAIL

NAME

ADDRESS

HOME

MOBILE

WORK / FAX

E-MAIL

NAME

ADDRESS

HOME

MOBILE

WORK / FAX

E-MAIL

NAME

ADDRESS

HOME

MOBILE

WORK / FAX

E-MAIL

NAME

ADDRESS

HOME

MOBILE

WORK / FAX

E-MAIL

NAME

ADDRESS

HOME

MOBILE

WORK / FAX

E-MAIL

Name

Address

Home

Mobile

Work / Fax

E-Mail

Name

Address

Home

Mobile

Work / Fax

E-Mail

Name

Address

Home

Mobile

Work / Fax

E-Mail

NAME

ADDRESS

HOME

MOBILE

WORK / FAX

E-MAIL

NAME

ADDRESS

HOME

MOBILE

WORK / FAX

E-MAIL

NAME

ADDRESS

HOME

MOBILE

WORK / FAX

E-MAIL

NAME

ADDRESS

HOME

MOBILE

WORK / FAX

E-MAIL

NAME

ADDRESS

HOME

MOBILE

WORK / FAX

E-MAIL

NAME

ADDRESS

HOME

MOBILE

WORK / FAX

E-MAIL

NAME

ADDRESS

HOME

MOBILE

WORK / FAX

E-MAIL

NAME

ADDRESS

HOME

MOBILE

WORK / FAX

E-MAIL

NAME

ADDRESS

HOME

MOBILE

WORK / FAX

E-MAIL

NAME

ADDRESS

HOME

MOBILE

WORK / FAX

E-MAIL

NAME

ADDRESS

HOME

MOBILE

WORK / FAX

E-MAIL

NAME

ADDRESS

HOME

MOBILE

WORK / FAX

E-MAIL

NAME

ADDRESS

HOME

MOBILE

WORK / FAX

E-MAIL

NAME

ADDRESS

HOME

MOBILE

WORK / FAX

E-MAIL

NAME

ADDRESS

HOME

MOBILE

WORK / FAX

E-MAIL

NAME

ADDRESS

HOME

MOBILE

WORK / FAX

E-MAIL

NAME

ADDRESS

HOME

MOBILE

WORK / FAX

E-MAIL

NAME

ADDRESS

HOME

MOBILE

WORK / FAX

E-MAIL

NAME

ADDRESS

HOME

MOBILE

WORK / FAX

E-MAIL

NAME

ADDRESS

HOME

MOBILE

WORK / FAX

E-MAIL

NAME

ADDRESS

HOME

MOBILE

WORK / FAX

E-MAIL

NAME

ADDRESS

HOME

MOBILE

WORK / FAX

E-MAIL

NAME

ADDRESS

HOME

MOBILE

WORK / FAX

E-MAIL

NAME

ADDRESS

HOME

MOBILE

WORK / FAX

E-MAIL

NAME

ADDRESS

HOME

MOBILE

WORK / FAX

E-MAIL

NAME

ADDRESS

HOME

MOBILE

WORK / FAX

E-MAIL

NAME

ADDRESS

HOME

MOBILE

WORK / FAX

E-MAIL

Name

Address

Home

Mobile

Work / Fax

E-Mail

Name

Address

Home

Mobile

Work / Fax

E-Mail

Name

Address

Home

Mobile

Work / Fax

E-Mail

Name

Address

Home

Mobile

Work / Fax

E-Mail

Name

Address

Home

Mobile

Work / Fax

E-Mail

Name

Address

Home

Mobile

Work / Fax

E-Mail

NAME

ADDRESS

HOME

MOBILE

WORK / FAX

E-MAIL

NAME

ADDRESS

HOME

MOBILE

WORK / FAX

E-MAIL

NAME

ADDRESS

HOME

MOBILE

WORK / FAX

E-MAIL

NAME

ADDRESS

HOME

MOBILE

WORK / FAX

E-MAIL

NAME

ADDRESS

HOME

MOBILE

WORK / FAX

E-MAIL

NAME

ADDRESS

HOME

MOBILE

WORK / FAX

E-MAIL

NAME

ADDRESS

HOME

MOBILE

WORK / FAX

E-MAIL

NAME

ADDRESS

HOME

MOBILE

WORK / FAX

E-MAIL

NAME

ADDRESS

HOME

MOBILE

WORK / FAX

E-MAIL

NAME

ADDRESS

HOME

MOBILE

WORK / FAX

E-MAIL

NAME

ADDRESS

HOME

MOBILE

WORK / FAX

E-MAIL

NAME

ADDRESS

HOME

MOBILE

WORK / FAX

E-MAIL

Name

Address

Home

Mobile

Work / Fax

E-Mail

Name

Address

Home

Mobile

Work / Fax

E-Mail

Name

Address

Home

Mobile

Work / Fax

E-Mail

NAME

ADDRESS

HOME

MOBILE

WORK / FAX

E-MAIL

NAME

ADDRESS

HOME

MOBILE

WORK / FAX

E-MAIL

NAME

ADDRESS

HOME

MOBILE

WORK / FAX

E-MAIL

NAME

ADDRESS

HOME

MOBILE

WORK / FAX

E-MAIL

NAME

ADDRESS

HOME

MOBILE

WORK / FAX

E-MAIL

NAME

ADDRESS

HOME

MOBILE

WORK / FAX

E-MAIL

NAME

ADDRESS

HOME

MOBILE

WORK / FAX

E-MAIL

NAME

ADDRESS

HOME

MOBILE

WORK / FAX

E-MAIL

NAME

ADDRESS

HOME

MOBILE

WORK / FAX

E-MAIL

NAME

ADDRESS

HOME

MOBILE

WORK / FAX

E-MAIL

NAME

ADDRESS

HOME

MOBILE

WORK / FAX

E-MAIL

NAME

ADDRESS

HOME

MOBILE

WORK / FAX

E-MAIL

NAME

ADDRESS

HOME

MOBILE

WORK / FAX

E-MAIL

NAME

ADDRESS

HOME

MOBILE

WORK / FAX

E-MAIL

NAME

ADDRESS

HOME

MOBILE

WORK / FAX

E-MAIL

W X

NAME

ADDRESS

HOME

MOBILE

WORK / FAX

E-MAIL

NAME

ADDRESS

HOME

MOBILE

WORK / FAX

E-MAIL

NAME

ADDRESS

HOME

MOBILE

WORK / FAX

E-MAIL

NAME

ADDRESS

HOME

MOBILE

WORK / FAX

E-MAIL

NAME

ADDRESS

HOME

MOBILE

WORK / FAX

E-MAIL

NAME

ADDRESS

HOME

MOBILE

WORK / FAX

E-MAIL

NAME

ADDRESS

HOME

MOBILE

WORK / FAX

E-MAIL

NAME

ADDRESS

HOME

MOBILE

WORK / FAX

E-MAIL

NAME

ADDRESS

HOME

MOBILE

WORK / FAX

E-MAIL

NAME

ADDRESS

HOME

MOBILE

WORK / FAX

E-MAIL

NAME

ADDRESS

HOME

MOBILE

WORK / FAX

E-MAIL

NAME

ADDRESS

HOME

MOBILE

WORK / FAX

E-MAIL

NAME

ADDRESS

HOME

MOBILE

WORK / FAX

E-MAIL

NAME

ADDRESS

HOME

MOBILE

WORK / FAX

E-MAIL

NAME

ADDRESS

HOME

MOBILE

WORK / FAX

E-MAIL

NAME

ADDRESS

HOME

MOBILE

WORK / FAX

E-MAIL

NAME

ADDRESS

HOME

MOBILE

WORK / FAX

E-MAIL

NAME

ADDRESS

HOME

MOBILE

WORK / FAX

E-MAIL

NAME

ADDRESS

HOME

MOBILE

WORK / FAX

E-MAIL

NAME

ADDRESS

HOME

MOBILE

WORK / FAX

E-MAIL

NAME

ADDRESS

HOME

MOBILE

WORK / FAX

E-MAIL

NAME

ADDRESS

HOME

MOBILE

WORK / FAX

E-MAIL

NAME

ADDRESS

HOME

MOBILE

WORK / FAX

E-MAIL

NAME

ADDRESS

HOME

MOBILE

WORK / FAX

E-MAIL

NAME

ADDRESS

HOME

MOBILE

WORK / FAX

E-MAIL

NAME

ADDRESS

HOME

MOBILE

WORK / FAX

E-MAIL

NAME

ADDRESS

HOME

MOBILE

WORK / FAX

E-MAIL

NAME

ADDRESS

HOME

MOBILE

WORK / FAX

E-MAIL

NAME

ADDRESS

HOME

MOBILE

WORK / FAX

E-MAIL

NAME

ADDRESS

HOME

MOBILE

WORK / FAX

E-MAIL

NAME

ADDRESS

HOME

MOBILE

WORK / FAX

E-MAIL

NAME

ADDRESS

HOME

MOBILE

WORK / FAX

E-MAIL

NAME

ADDRESS

HOME

MOBILE

WORK / FAX

E-MAIL

NAME

ADDRESS

HOME

MOBILE

WORK / FAX

E-MAIL

NAME

ADDRESS

HOME

MOBILE

WORK / FAX

E-MAIL

NAME

ADDRESS

HOME

MOBILE

WORK / FAX

E-MAIL

NAME

ADDRESS

HOME

MOBILE

WORK / FAX

E-MAIL

NAME

ADDRESS

HOME

MOBILE

WORK / FAX

E-MAIL

NAME

ADDRESS

HOME

MOBILE

WORK / FAX

E-MAIL

Y
Z

NAME

ADDRESS

HOME

MOBILE

WORK / FAX

E-MAIL

NAME

ADDRESS

HOME

MOBILE

WORK / FAX

E-MAIL

NAME

ADDRESS

HOME

MOBILE

WORK / FAX

E-MAIL